ANIMAL CHAMPIONS

Published by Creative Education, Inc., 123 South Broad Street, Mankato, Minnesota 56001

Library of Congress Cataloging-in-Publication Data

Wexo, John Bonnett.
Animal champions / by John Bonnett Wexo.
p.   cm. — (Zoobooks)
Summary: Discusses unusual animals which stand out for their abilities or appearance.
ISBN 0-88682-409-5
1. Animals—Miscellanea—Juvenile literature. [1. Animals—Miscellanea.] I. Title. II. Series: Zoo books (Mankato, Minn.)
QL49.W48   1991   591—dc20   91-11775 CIP AC

ANIMAL CHAMPIONS

Zoobook Series Created by
John Bonnett Wexo

Written by
John Bonnett Wexo

Zoological Consultant
Charles R. Schroeder, D.V.M.
Director Emeritus
San Diego Zoo &
San Diego Wild Animal Park

MEDIA LIBRARY
Piney Orchard
Elementary School

Creative Education

Photographic Credits

Cover: H.J. Fluëgel (Bruce Coleman, Ltd.); **Pages Six and Seven:** Background Photo, Michael Freeman (Bruce Coleman, Ltd.); **Page Six: Top,** Stephen Dalton (Natuarl History Photographic Agency); **Left Center,** Sven Lindblad (Photo Researchers); **Lower Right,** Kenneth Fink (Bruce Coleman, Inc.); **Page Seven: Top,** Wayne Lankinen (DRK Photo); **Left Center,** Anthony Mercieca (Shostal & Assoc.); **Lower Left,** G. Ziesler (Peter Arnold, Inc.); **Lower Right,** Zig Leszczynski (Animals Animals); **Pages Eight and Nine:** Jen & Des Bartlett (Bruce Coleman, Inc.); **Pages Ten and Eleven: Background Photo,** Leonard Lee Rue III (Alpha/FPG); **Page Ten: Top,** Francisco Erize (Bruce Coleman, Inc.); **Center,** Francisco Erize (Bruce Coleman, Inc.); **Lower Left,** Wayne Lankinen (DRK Photo); **Lower Right,** Bob McKeever (Tom Stack & Assoc.); **Page Eleven: Top Left,** M.P. Kahl (Bruce Coleman, Ltd); **Top Center,** E.R. Degginger; **Top Right,** Dieter & Mary Plage (Bruce Coleman, Ltd.); **Center,** C.B. Frith (Bruce Coleman, Ltd.); **Lower Right,** Tom McHugh (Photo Researchers); **Pages Twelve and Thirteen:** Francois Gohier (Ardea London); **Page Fourteen: Top,** P. Morris (Ardea London); **Left Center,** A.D. Trounson & M.C. Clampett (Ardea London); **Right Center,** Wardene Weisser (Bruce Coleman, Inc.); **Lower Left,** M.B.L. Fogden (Bruce Coleman, Ltd.); **Page Fifteen: Top Left,** George Holton (Photo Researchers); **Top Right,** J. Grant (Natural Science Photos); **Lower Left,** W.E. Townsend, Jr. (Bruce Coleman, Ltd.); **Lower Right,** John Chellman (Animals Animals); **Pages Sixteen and Seventeen:** Michael Dick (Animals Animals); **Page Eighteen: Top Right,** Hans & Judy Beste (Animals Animals); **Center,** Peter Davey (Bruce Coleman, Inc.); **Lower Left,** Jen & Des Bartlett (Bruce Coleman, Inc.); **Page Nineteen: Top Left,** Tom McHugh (Photo Researchers); **Top Right,** Ken Balcomb (Bruce Coleman, Ltd.); **Center,** P.H. Ward (Natural Science Photos); **Lower Left,** E.R. Degginger (Animals Animals); **Lower Right,** Peter Parks (Animals Animals); **Page Twenty: Top Right,** Francis Gohier (Ardea London); **Lower Left,** Ron Austing (Photo Researchers); **Lower Right,** John R. Lewis (Tom Stack & Assoc.); **Page Twenty-one: Top Left,** Russ Kinne (Photo Researchers); **Top Right,** S.J. Krasemann (Peter Arnold, Inc.); **Center,** David C. Fritts (Animals Animals); **Lower Center,** David Hughes (Bruce Coleman, Ltd.); **Page Twenty-two and Inside Back Cover:** Ranjitsinh (Animals Animals).

Our Thanks To: Alex Saikowski, Rick Perrelet (Photovisions); Janet Lombard, Michaele Robinson (San Diego Zoo Library); Susan Hensley (San Diego Technical Books); Salvador Tarango (Frye & Smith); Marvin Jones (San Diego Zoo).

Contents

Animal champions are much like human champions—there is something about them that makes them stand out from the rest. Some of them run, swim, or fly faster than other animals. Others can jump higher, dive deeper, or travel farther. A few are champions because they live the longest, grow the tallest, weigh the most, or are simply the strongest.

Animal champions set records just like human athletes do. But it is much harder to measure these records, because they are set in wild places where it is difficult to get accurate measurements. For this reason, most of the records you see in this book are approximate. They are the best guesses that scientists can make.

On these two pages, we show some of the fastest creatures in the animal world. As you read about them, remember that top speed for human runners is 20–25 miles per hour (32–40 kilometers per hour). And humans can only run at this speed for a few hundred yards.

The honey bee is tiny compared to a human. But it can fly almost as fast as a human runs. It beats its wings an incredible 15,000 times every minute!

Heavy people do not run very fast. But some heavy animals can run with amazing speed. Elephants can charge at 25 miles per hour (40 kilometers per hour). And black rhinos can run nearly 30 miles per hour (48 kilometers per hour), even though they may weigh over 3,500 pounds (1,588 kilograms).

We don't think of ducks as being very fast. But canvasback ducks can fly more than 70 miles per hour (113 kilometers per hour) when migrating.

Pronghorn antelope are the fastest land animals over long distances. They can run at a steady speed of 35 miles per hour (56 kilometers per hour) for many miles. Their top speed is probably more than 50 miles per hour (80 kilometers per hour).

When diving, peregrine falcons may reach speeds of 200 miles per hour (322 kilometers per hour). When flying level, peregrines have been timed at 60 miles per hour (97 kilometers per hour).

Hummingbirds move their wings faster than any other birds. Some of them beat their wings 500 times per minute.

The cheetah is the fastest mammal. It can run faster than 70 miles per hour (113 kilometers per hour). But it gets tired quickly and usually stops after a few hundred yards.

For its size, the female house spider is much faster than a cheetah. It can run *330 times* the length of its own body in 10 seconds. To match this, a cheetah would have to run faster than 115 miles per hour (185 kilometers per hour)!

Ostriches can't fly, but they can run faster than any other bird and most other animals as well. They can reach speeds of up to 35 miles per hour (56 kilometers per hour), and keep it up for 20 miles (32 kilometers). They are also the largest of all birds, and they lay the largest eggs.

Size is something we usually judge by our own size. If an animal is bigger than a person, we say it is a big animal. If it is smaller than a person, we say it is a small animal. But we should really judge the size of an animal by *what kind of animal* it is. For instance, a beetle that weighs 3½ ounces (100 grams) may seem very small to us—but it is a giant in the insect world.

Also, when you are talking about size in the animal world, you must remember *what kind of size* you are talking about. For instance, the African elephant is the *heaviest* land animal in the world. But giraffes are *taller*. Reticulated pythons are *longer*. And, if we count their wingspan, albatrosses are *wider*. In a way, they are *all* the largest.

More than half of all living mammals are *rodents*. This group includes rats, mice, squirrels, chipmunks, woodchucks, gophers, porcupines, and beavers. The largest of all rodents is the capybara of South America, also called the "water hog." These huge relatives of mice can be 4½ feet long (137 centimeters), and may weigh almost 150 pounds (68 kilograms.)

The heaviest land animal on record is an African elephant. It weighed more than 24,000 pounds (10,886 kilograms)

The largest meat-eating land animals are the polar bear and the kodiak bear. In 1960, a huge polar bear was measured after it had been killed by a hunter. It stood 11½ feet tall (3.5 meters) and weighed 2,210 pounds (1,002 kilograms).

Goliath beetles are the heaviest insects on earth. They can weigh more than 3½ ounces (100 grams)—approximately 200 times more than a house fly.

The title of "tallest land animal" goes to the giraffe. The greatest height ever recorded for a giraffe is 19 feet 3 inches (5.9 meters).

Kori bustards are the heaviest of all flying birds. The record weight for a kori bustard is 40 pounds (18 kilograms).

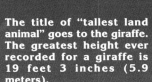

Reticulated pythons are the giants of the snake world. They can be over 28 feet long (8.5 meters).

wandering albatross has the gest wings of any bird. The rd wingspan for this bird is feet 4 inches (3.5 meters).

Komodo dragons are the largest of all lizards. They can be 9 feet long (2.7 meters) and can weigh more than 200 pounds (91 kilograms).

Saltwater crocodiles are the biggest reptiles in the world. The largest ever measured was 25½ feet long (7.9 meters) and probably weighed over 4,000 pounds (1,814 kilograms).

Whales are the largest and among the most graceful of mammals. They make haunting "music" underwater that can be heard for great distances. Legend says that humpback whales can actually hear each other over a space of a thousand miles, but we do not yet know their limits for certain.

HUMPBACK WHALE

Long life is something we also judge by comparing it to human age. If an animal lives longer than most people do, we say it has a long life. But very few animals outlive humans. The oldest human on record lived 117 years, and not many animals can match that. So we don't think animals live very long, as a rule.

But again, we should really judge the age of an animal according to the group it belongs to, not according to human age. For instance, most insects live less than 1 year, so an insect that lives 50 years is really very old. It lives *50 times longer* than the average insect. If you could live 50 times longer than the average human, you would live to be 3,500 years old!

The longest-living fish is probably the lake sturgeon. These strange-looking creatures may live to be more than 80 years old.

Some birds live a very long time. But it's hard to tell which bird lives the longest, because the ages are difficult to prove. Some people say that a sulfer-crested cockatoo (like the one shown at left) lived more than 120 years. But there is no way to prove this claim. The oldest age that has been proven is 72 years for an Andean condor (like the one shown at right). This bird lived its entire life in a zoo.

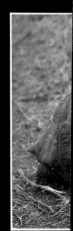

Queen termites can live and lay eggs for more than 50 years. And some scientists believe that they can live over 100 years.

Gorillas can live a long time, but nobody is sure just how long. The oldest known gorilla is still alive. He is 52 years old and lives in a zoo.

Wild donkeys are hardy animals and can live 47 years. Domestic horses can live even longer—as many as 62 years.

Giant tortoises can live more than 150 years. Some tortoises living today were hatched before the Civil War.

"Hippopotamus" is a Greek word meaning "river horse." Of course, hippos aren't really horses. But they can live nearly as long as a horse—49 years.

Some species of tree frogs can leap
a distance a hundred times their
body length by "sailing" from one
tree branch to another, much like a
flying squirrel.

GIANT TREE FROG

Strength and agility are two of the most important qualities for human athletes. Many human champions take pride in their ability to lift great amounts of weight. The strongest human can lift 600 pounds (272 kilograms)—about two times his own weight. But, as you will see, some animals can do even better than that. For example, there are insects that can lift *50 times* their own weight.

The highest that any human has ever jumped is 7 feet 8¾ inches (2.4 meters). With a pole to help them, some humans can jump as high as 19 feet (5.8 meters) —about three times their own height. But there is an insect that can do *66 times* better than that, without using a pole!

When it comes to diving, the deepest that any human has gone is 285 feet (86.9 meters). And the longest that any person has held his breath under water is about 13¾ minutes. But there is an air-breathing mammal that can dive *37 times* deeper and hold its breath *18 times* longer.

In one hop, a grey kangaroo can jump a distance of 44 feet (13.4 meters). And when it really gets going, it can leap more than 11 feet (3.4 meters) off the ground.

Chimpanzees are only about half as tall as humans, but they are three times stronger. They can lift six times their own body weight.

The strongest land animal of all is the Asiatic elephant. It can lift more than a ton with its trunk (907 kilograms). And it can drag a load weighing over *20,000 pounds* (9,070 kilograms).

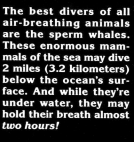

The best divers of all air-breathing animals are the sperm whales. These enormous mammals of the sea may dive 2 miles (3.2 kilometers) below the ocean's surface. And while they're under water, they may hold their breath almost *two hours!*

The tiny kangaroo rat is named for its jumping ability. It is actually a better jumper than the gray kangaroo. The gray kangaroo jumps eight times the length of its body—but the kangaroo rat can jump *48 times* its own length.

Some ants can lift *50 times* their own weight—and they do it with their jaws.

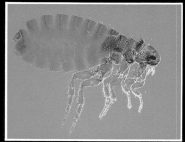

The high-jumping champion of the cat family is the puma. One of these magnificent cats was seen jumping 18 feet (5.5 meters) straight up in the air.

For its size, the common flea is the greatest jumper of them all. It can jump *200 times* its own height. And a hungry flea can jump 10,000 times an hour.

rathon **runners** are proud of
ability to run long distances. They
ver 26 miles (42 kilometers) without
ping. But many animals travel much
er. They may go thousands of miles
rch of food or to escape bad weather.
some journey long distances to find
places to raise their young.

hen animals take regular trips every
to do these things, their movements
lled *migrations*. During these migra-
they show a determination and en-
ce that we can only admire. Nothing
s to stand in their way. Many of them
wide oceans or barren wastelands.
rs fly over the highest mountains.
some may swim up the fastest rushing
ms. Quite remarkably, these animals
find their way across oceans, moun-
anges, and vast wildernesses without
p to guide them!

The greatest travelers in the mammal family are the
California gray whales. Every year, these huge animals
migrate 26,000 miles (42,000 kilometers) from feeding
grounds to breeding grounds, and back again. They
swim about 115 miles a day (185 kilometers).

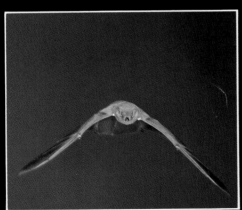

The red bat is the champion flyer among
the mammals. Every year it migrates more
than 5,600 miles (9,000 kilometers). And
most of that journey is over the ocean.

Siberian tigers often wander great distances
in search of food. One big male walked more

they were hatched to lay their eggs. To make this journey, a Chinook salmon may swim as many as 3,000 miles (4,827 kilometers).

Arctic terns are probably the greatest travelers among the birds. They may fly 20,000 miles (32,000 kilometers) in a single year—a distance equal to a trip around the world.

Caribou often migrate long distances between their winter and summer homes. To get from one home to the other, they may travel 800 miles (1,287 kilometers). Along the way, they often have to cross water. They can swim at a speed of 6 miles per hour (9.7 kilometers per hour).

To lay their eggs, green sea turtles return every year to the place where they were hatched. To do this, some of them may swim 2,800 miles (4,505 kilometers).

Bar-headed geese are probably the highest flying birds. They have been seen flying over the top of Mount Everest at an altitude of 29,028 feet (8,848 meters)—more than *5½ miles* up in the air (8.8 kilometers).

Index